PHON
Crosspatches

book 3

COPYRIGHT INFORMATION

This master may only be reproduced by the
original purchaser for use with their class(es).
The publisher prohibits the loaning or onselling
of this master for purposes of reproduction.

Prim-Ed
Publishing

CW00457422

Phonic Crosspatches Book 3
Prim-Ed Publishing
Centenary Business Centre
Hammond Close
Attleborough Fields Industrial Estate
Nuneaton CV116RY
Fax: (0203) 642402

ISBN 1 86311 106 9
ISBN 1 86311 107 7 Set
0233

First Published in 1990 by R.I.C. Publications.

Revised and reprinted under license in 1994
by Prim-Ed Publishing.

Copyright 1990 by R.I.C. Publications.

This master may only be reproduced by the original
purchaser for use with their class(es) only.
The publisher prohibits the loaning or onselling of
this master for the purposes of reproduction.

Other copy master titles available from Prim-Ed Publishing include:

Mathematics

0031-0033	Chance, Statistics and Graphs (3 Levels)
0061-0063	Beginning Maths (3 Books)
0211	My Number Fold-a-Book
0601-0603	Problem Solving with Mathematics (3 Levels)
0610	How to use a Calculator
0612	Step into Tables
0620-0622	Exploring Time (3 Levels)
0064-0066	Problem Solving Through Investigation (3 Levels)

Language

0108-0110	Cloze (3 Levels)
0117-0119	Comprehend It! (3 Levels)
0121-0123	Comprehension (3 Levels)
0131-0133	Phonics (3 Levels)
0134	The Big Book of Phonics
0161-0163	Language Through Reading (3 Books)
0170	Dictionary Skills
0231-0233	Phonic Crosspatches (3 Books)
0291-0293	Problem Solving with Language (3 Levels)
0210	My Alphabet Fold-a-Book
2007-2009	Active Comprehension (3 Levels)
2010-2013	Write Creatively (4 Levels)
2014-2019	Word Attack! (6 Levels)

Social Studies

0301-0303	Mapping Skills (3 Levels)
0350	Continents of the World
0351	Mountains of the World
0352	Waterways of the World

Science

0508-0510	Design & Technology (3 Levels)

Lower Primary Themes

0451	Witches
0452	Frogs
0453	Giants
0454	Pirates
0455	Dragons
0464	Dinosaurs
0461	The Big Book of Christmas

General Studies

0320	The Environment and Us
0321	The Green Book
0429	Contracts
0428	Finding Your Way

Copyright Notice

Blackline masters or copy masters are published and sold with a limited copyright. This copyright allows publishers to provide teachers and schools with a wide range of learning activities without copyright being breached. This limited copyright allows the purchaser to make sufficient copies for use within their own education institution. The copyright is not transferable, nor can it be onsold. Following these instructions is not essential but will ensure that you, as the purchaser, have evidence of legal ownership to the copyright if inspection occurs.

For your added protection in the case of copyright inspection, please complete the form below. Retain this form, the complete original document and the invoice or receipt as proof of purchase.

Name of Purchaser: _____

Date of Purchase: _____

Supplier: _____

School Order # (if applicable): _____

Signature of Purchaser: _____

9.50

Book 3

PHONIC
Crosspatches

Published by
Prim-Ed Publishing

Foreword

This series of three blackline master books are designed as a supplement and reinforcement resource to the teaching of phonics. The books have been graded according to phonic types, but they do progress in difficulty from Book 1 through to Book 3. The size of the crosspatch squares have been designed to accommodate large printing and the artwork used reflects the content of each page.

All words to be used are given however, if the teacher desires they can be covered easily before photocopying.

CONTENTS

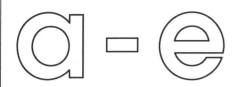

Name _____

lake	grape	spade	plane
whale	snake	game	cake

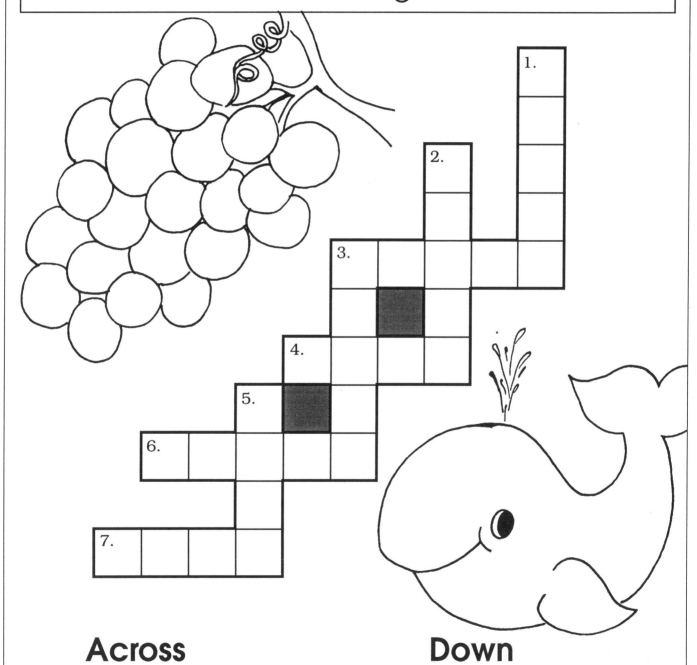

Across

3. You dig with it
4. Made of water
6. A large ocean animal
7. Baked in an oven

Down

1. It can fly
2. A fruit
3. Has no legs
5. Chess is a ....

Name _____

sneeze	tree	cheese	thirteen
cheep	free	see	freeze

Across

4. To make very cold
7. Costing nothing
8. Happens during a cold

Down

1. After twelve
2. Wood comes from this
3. Made from milk
5. A bird noise
6. I can .... with my eyes

ie

| lied | tie | died | cried |
| pie | die | tied | fried |

Across

2. To stop living
4. To be cooked in oil
5. She ..... her shoe laces
6. A meat ....

Down

1. The boy .... to me
2. He .... in the accident
3. He ...... after being burnt
5. Worn around the neck

i - e

smile	time	pipe	dive
slide	hide	hive	like

Across

3. A bee's home
5. .... and seek
7. Found in the playground

Down

1. Kept by a watch
2. I .... ice-cream
4. I like to .... into water
6. A water ....
7. Makes a happy face

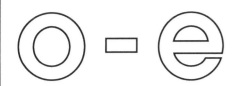

Name _____

| home | rope | rode | drove |
| stone | throne | slope | stove |

Across

1. Used on sailing ships
3. Very hard
6. A king's chair
7. You live in it

Down

1. They .... their bikes
2. A ski ....
4. Used for cooking
5. We .... to the shops

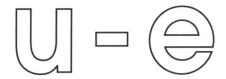

Name _____

| prune | June | mute | pollute |
| rude | flute | ruler | salute |

Across

4. Bad mannered
6. To make dirty
7. A month of the year

Down

1. Making no sound
2. A musical instrument
3. What soldiers do
5. Helps draw straight lines
6. A dried plum

oa

Name _____

coach	croak	goat	float
coat	cloak		

Across

2. An animal
3. You wear it
4. Pulled by horses

Down

1. Opposite to sink
3. The sound a frog makes
5. Like a coat

Name _____

oil   coil   soil   spoil

coin   boil   moist   noise

Across

2. A form of money
5. Another word for damp
6. Used in cars
8. To ruin

Down

1. A very painful sore
3. A loud ....
4. To curl up
7. You grow plants in it

room	broom	droop	tooth
spoon	boot	moon	food

Across

2. A place in the home
5. To bend over
6. You put it on your foot
7. Seen mostly at night

Down

1. You eat it
3. Found in your mouth
4. You eat with it
6. Used for sweeping

OU

cloud	mouse	house	found
loud	couch	round	sound

Across

2. A place to sit
4. Opposite to lost
6. A small animal
8. Seen in the sky

Down

1. Like a circle
3. You live in one
5. A loud ....
7. A .... bark

ai

Name _____

rain	mail	paint	chain
nail	train	stain	sail

Across

3. Comes in the post
6. Runs on rails
7. Made from steel
8. Comes from the sky

Down

1. Part of a ship
2. Found on a bike
4. A dirty mark
5. Brightly coloured

Name _____

| peach | seat | sea | clean |
| steam | speak | meat | seam |

Across

2. Part of a dress
5. Very hot
6. A place for boats
7. You wash to keep ....

Down

1. You can rest in one
3. You can eat it
4. A fruit
5. .... quietly

air

fair	dairy	chair	stair
pair	fairy	hair	aircraft

Across

3. Found on your head
5. A machine that can fly
6. A small creature
7. A .... of shoes

Down

1. I went up the ....case
2. You sit on it
4. A place for cows
6. Light-coloured

stall   fall   call   small

Across

3. Opposite to large
4. Opposite to climb

Down

1. A place where horses are kept
2. To speak loudly

alk

Name _____

talk	walk	balk	chalk
stalk	beanstalk		

Across

3. Jack and the ....
5. To speak
6. Slower than a run

Down

1. To pretend
2. Used on a blackboard
4. Part of a plant

Name _____

| year | gear | tear | shear |
| fear | near | hear | appear |

Across

2. To feel frightened
4. Close to
5. To cut off
8. I forgot my cricket ....

Down

1. Caused by crying
3. 365 days make a ....
6. I can .... the music
7. To be seen

Name _____

pour	colour	your	neighbour
four	course	court	source

Across

3. To tip out or .... water
5. Your next door ....
6. It was a three -...... meal
7. A tennis ....

Down

1. Bring .... own lunch
2. A number
4. The beginning
6. Red is a ....

wor

workshop   work   word   worst
bookworm   worth   world   earthworm

Across

1. The earth and all life
4. A place to work
5. Its value
6. Made from letters

Down

1. Very bad
2. Lives in the earth
3. A lover of books
4. A job

b

Name _____

lamb	bomb	thumb	crumb
limb	numb	comb	climb

Across

2. An arm or leg
4. A bread ....
5. It can blow up
6. Feeling no pain

Down

1. .... your hair
2. A baby sheep
3. Part of the hand
4. To .... a tree

kn

knee	knit	knot	knuckle
knew	know	knock	knife

Across

2. I don't ..... the answer
4. Part of the hand
6. He .... the answer
7. I can .... a jumper

Down

1. To tie a ....
2. Part of the leg
3. Used for cutting
5. A .... on the door

a

path	past	bath	glass
basket	last	father	castle

Across

4. Used to carry things
5. Opposite to first
6. The soldiers marched .....

Down

1. A large stone building
2. .... and mother
3. Hard and clear
4. Is filled with water
6. You walk along a ....

Name _____

dove	glove	shovel	nothing
monkey	Monday	money	sponge

Across

2. Used to buy things
5. I have .... left
7. Soaks up water

Down

1. A small bird
2. A day of the week
3. An animal
4. Used for digging
6. Put on hands

| polo | post | pony | volcano |
| hello | melody | tomato | clover |

Across

2. A lamp ....
5. A tune
6. A type of grass
8. A red fruit

Down

1. A small horse
3. A greeting
4. A mountain of 'fire'
7. A sport that uses horses

ce - cy

cent	fence	palace	celery
prince	cellar	cymbol	bicycle

Across

3. Used in music
4. Part of a dollar
5. It has two wheels
8. Keeps things in or out

Down

1. Where kings or queens live
2. .... Charming
6. A vegetable
7. Room beneath a house

ice-ace

| face | race | place | disgrace |
| spice | nice | rice | twice |

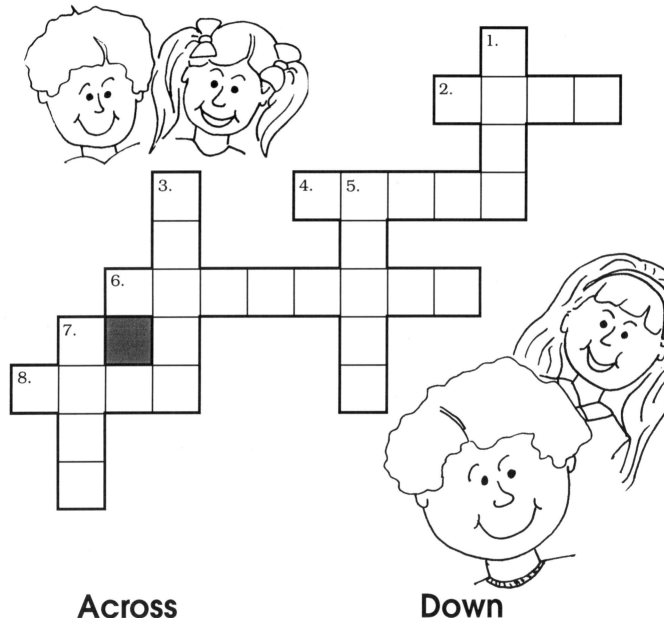

Across

2. A happy ....
4. Added to food for taste
6. To shame
8. Very pleasant

Down

1. A contest
3. Two times
5. An open space or square
7. A seed that is eaten

ge-gi

Name _____

cage	rage	page	cabbage
stage	magic	giant	engine

Across

2. Part of a book
3. Part of a theatre
6. A vegetable
8. A bird ....

Down

1. An angry mood
4. A very large person
5. Part of a car
7. A .... trick